Piano/Vocal Selections

Fiorello!
A New Musical

FAY GAGE

T0087790

Contents

ISBN 1-4234-1031-9

HAL•LEONARD®
CORPORATION

7777 W. BLUEMOUND RD. P.O. BOX 13819 MILWAUKEE, WI 53213

Visit Hal Leonard Online at
www.halleonard.com

'TIL TOMORROW

Words by SHELDON HARNICK
Music by JERRY BOCK

GENTLEMAN JIMMY

Words by SHELDON HARNICK
Music by JERRY BOCK

Charleston

Verse

Live and let live___ love and let love___ There are no

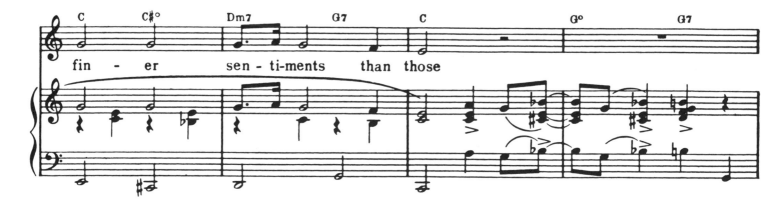

fin - er sen - ti-ments than those

Live and let live___ love and let love___

(I'll Marry)
THE VERY NEXT MAN

Words by SHELDON HARNICK
Music by JERRY BOCK

WHEN DID I FALL IN LOVE

Words by SHELDON HARNICK
Music by JERRY BOCK

I LOVE A COP

Words by SHELDON HARNICK
Music by JERRY BOCK

POLITICS AND POKER

Words by SHELDON HARNICK
Music by JERRY BOCK

WHERE DO I GO FROM HERE

Words by SHELDON HARNICK
Music by JERRY BOCK

LITTLE TIN BOX

Words by SHELDON HARNICK
Music by JERRY BOCK

24